Would You Rather
MAD LIBS

by Olivia Luchini

MAD LIBS
An imprint of Penguin Random House LLC, New York

First published in the United States of America by Mad Libs,
an imprint of Penguin Random House LLC, New York, 2024

Mad Libs format and text copyright © 2024 by Penguin Random House LLC

Concept created by Roger Price & Leonard Stern

Cover illustration by Scott Brooks

MAD LIBS and logo are registered trademarks of Penguin Random House LLC.

Visit us online at penguinrandomhouse.com.

Printed in the United States of America

ISBN 9780593658628
1 3 5 7 9 10 8 6 4 2
COMR

MAD⊙LIBS
WOULD YOU RATHER

INSTRUCTIONS

WOULD YOU RATHER MAD LIBS® is a game you play by filling in different types of words to complete a series of silly WOULD-YOU-RATHER QUESTIONS.

To play alone: Pick a chapter in the book and then complete the blank spaces for each WOULD-YOU-RATHER QUESTION. Decide which option you would prefer if you had to choose! Then, pick your favorite WOULD-YOU-RATHER for the whole chapter!

To play in a group: Pick a chapter in the book. Then, choose one person in the group to be the READER. The READER asks the group for words to fill in the blank spaces of one WOULD-YOU-RATHER QUESTION in the chapter—without letting the group see the question!

The READER writes the suggested words in the blank spaces, reads the completed WOULD-YOU-RATHER QUESTION out loud to the group, then asks each member of the group to guess which WOULD-YOU-RATHER option they think the READER would pick. The READER then reveals which option they would choose, and each member of the group who guessed right gets one point.

The READER then passes the book to another player so they can be the READER, and the game repeats with a new WOULD-YOU-RATHER QUESTION. At the end of the chapter, the player with the most points wins!

In case you have forgotten what adjectives, adverbs, nouns, and verbs are, here is a quick review:

An **ADJECTIVE** describes something or somebody. *Lumpy, soft, ugly, messy,* and *short* are adjectives.

An **ADVERB** tells how something is done. It modifies a verb and usually ends in "ly." *Modestly, stupidly, greedily,* and *carefully* are adverbs.

A **NOUN** is the name of a person, place, or thing. *Sidewalk, umbrella, bridle, bathtub,* and *nose* are nouns.

A **VERB** is an action word. *Run, pitch, jump,* and *swim* are verbs. Put the verbs in past tense if the directions say **PAST TENSE**. *Ran, pitched, jumped,* and *swam* are verbs in the past tense.

When we ask for **A PLACE**, we mean any sort of place: a country or city (*Spain, Cleveland*) or a room (*bathroom, kitchen*).

An **EXCLAMATION** or **SILLY WORD** is any sort of funny sound, gasp, grunt, or outcry, like *Wow!, Ouch!, Whomp!, Ick!,* and *Gadzooks!*

When we ask for specific words, like a **NUMBER**, a **COLOR**, an **ANIMAL**, or a **PART OF THE BODY**, we mean a word that is one of those things, like *seven, blue, horse,* or *head*.

When we ask for a **PLURAL**, it means more than one. For example, *cat* pluralized is *cats*.

WOULD YOU?

Here are some classic would-you-rather questions. Good luck! You'll need it.

Would you rather

wake up tomorrow and find out it's _____
NUMBER

years in the future

or

wake up tomorrow and realize you've gone back in

time _____ years?
NUMBER

Would you rather

find a/an _____ _____ under your
ADJECTIVE   SOMETHING ALIVE

bed

or

find a/an _____-breathing _____
NOUN   ANIMAL

in your closet?

Would you rather

work a summer job cleaning _____ for
                                PLURAL NOUN

a famous _____
              OCCUPATION

or

work a summer job polishing _____
                                  PLURAL NOUN

for _____ ?
        CELEBRITY

Would you rather

live on a/an _____ in outer space
                  NOUN

or

live underwater in a/an _____ ?
                            VEHICLE

Would you rather

_____ like a/an _____ in front of
    VERB   ANIMAL

a thousand strangers

or

juggle sharp _____ in front of
           PLURAL NOUN

_____ strangers?
    NUMBER

Would you rather

have a best friend who is also a/an _____
                                  ADJECTIVE

show-off

or

have a best friend who _____ every
                   VERB ENDING IN "S"

time you play a game?

GAMER AT WORK

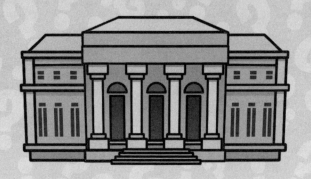

Would you rather

be locked in your favorite _____ for
TYPE OF BUILDING

two months

or

be allowed to go anywhere except your bedroom

for _____ years?
NUMBER

Would you rather

give _____ the ability to read your mind
PERSON YOU KNOW

or

give _____ the ability to control your
CELEBRITY

_____ ?
PART OF THE BODY

Would you rather

be able to _____ like a bird
<small>VERB</small>

or

swim like a/an _____ ?
<small>ANIMAL</small>

Would you rather

only be able to go on www. _____ .com
<small>NOUN</small>

or

be able to go on any website except

www. _____ .com?
<small>VERB</small>

DECISIONS! DECISIONS!

There are so many choices to make in life.
Here are a few more!

Would you rather

have to wear a/an _____ _____
ADJECTIVE   ARTICLE OF CLOTHING

for the rest of your life

or

have to balance a/an _____ on your
NOUN

_____ for the rest of your life?
PART OF THE BODY

Would you rather

play a game called "pin the _____ on
NOUN

the _____"
ANIMAL

or

play a game called "musical _____"?
PLURAL NOUN

Would you rather

_____ in a pool filled with _____
  VERB   TYPE OF LIQUID

or

climb a/an _____ made of _____
            NOUN   TYPE OF FOOD

that's two thousand feet tall?

Would you rather

run a mile in _____ -degree heat
               NUMBER

or

run _____ miles in perfect weather?
    NUMBER

Would you rather

get a dollar every time you _____
                             VERB

a/an _____
     NOUN

or

get a dollar every time you _____
                             VERB

a/an _____ ?
     TYPE OF FOOD

Would you rather

be best friends with a/an _____
ADJECTIVE

_____ forever
OCCUPATION

or

be friends with a/an _____ _____
ADJECTIVE   SOMETHING ALIVE

forever?

Would you rather

be as tall as a/an _____
NOUN

or

as _____ as a/an _____?
ADJECTIVE   NOUN

Would you rather

be a/an _____ who lives in a/an _____
ANIMAL   NOUN

or

be a/an _____ that lives in a/an
SOMETHING ALIVE

_____?
TYPE OF BUILDING

Would you rather

learn to _____ like a/an _____
           VERB   OCCUPATION

or

become an expert at _____
                           VERB ENDING IN "ING"

_____ ?
PLURAL NOUN

Would you rather

wear the same _____ for a whole month
               ARTICLE OF CLOTHING

or

not wear any _____ for a whole
            ARTICLE OF CLOTHING (PLURAL)

month?

Would you rather

live alone in a/an _____ _____
               ADJECTIVE   TYPE OF BUILDING

or

live with _____ in a/an _____ house?
    PERSON YOU KNOW   ADJECTIVE

Would you rather

bounce on a/an _____ full of _____
            NOUN   PLURAL NOUN

all day

or

swim in a/an _____ full of _____
         TYPE OF CONTAINER   TYPE OF LIQUID

all day?

Would you rather

go to (the) _____ with _____
              A PLACE   PERSON YOU KNOW

or

go to (the) _____ alone?
              A PLACE

Would you rather

only watch _____ for the rest of your life
              MOVIE TITLE

or

only listen to "_____" for the rest of your life?
                 SONG TITLE

Would you rather

be a superhero who can _____ _____
VERB   PLURAL NOUN

or

be a superhero who is as _____ as
ADJECTIVE

a/an _____ ?
NOUN

Would you rather

share a hug with a/an

_____ _____
ADJECTIVE   ANIMAL

or

shake hands with a/an _____ _____ ?
ADJECTIVE   ANIMAL

Would you rather

always smell like _____
TYPE OF FOOD

or

have the world around you smell like _____ ?
TYPE OF FOOD

Would you rather

sit lost on an iceberg while only wearing

a/an _____
ARTICLE OF CLOTHING

or

be lost on a/an _____ island with
ADJECTIVE

no _____ ?
PLURAL NOUN

Would you rather

write a book about _____ that is
PLURAL NOUN

_____ words long
NUMBER

or

read a/an _____ book by _____ that
ADJECTIVE   CELEBRITY

is all about _____ ?
OCCUPATION (PLURAL)

THIS OR THAT OR THIS

Pick the one you like best! There are no wrong answers. Or are there?

Would you rather

be _____ minutes early
        NUMBER

or

be _____ minutes late?
        NUMBER

Would you rather

find a hungry _____ in your favorite
                 ANIMAL

_____
A PLACE

or

find a/an _____ sleeping on your favorite
          SOMETHING ALIVE

_____?
NOUN

Would you rather

get a headache every time you _____
VERB

or

get a headache every time you see

a/an _____ ?
NOUN

Would you rather

be a/an _____ who has to wear
OCCUPATION

_____ -heel shoes
ADJECTIVE

or

be a/an _____ _____ who has to
ADJECTIVE   _OCCUPATION_

work barefoot?

Would you rather

fight ten _____ _____
ADJECTIVE   _ANIMAL (PLURAL)_

or

fight one _____ _____ ?
ADJECTIVE   _ANIMAL_

Would you rather

talk _____ all the time
ADVERB

or

walk _____ all the time?
ADVERB

Would you rather

look _____ in every selfie you take
ADJECTIVE

or

look _____ in every photo someone else
ADJECTIVE

takes of you?

Would you rather

_____ a/an _____ cat
VERB   ADJECTIVE

or

pet a/an _____ dog?
ADJECTIVE

Would you rather

live on top of a/an _____ in the middle
NOUN

of _____
COUNTRY

or

live in a/an _____ _____ in
ADJECTIVE   TYPE OF BUILDING

your hometown?

Would you rather

_____ every time someone says hello to you
VERB

or

_____ every time someone says your name?
VERB

Would you rather

have _____ play you in a movie about your life
CELEBRITY

or

play _____ in a movie about their life?
CELEBRITY

Would you rather

change your name to _____
SILLY WORD

or

change your name to _____
FIRST NAME

_____ . Mc- _____ -face?
LETTER OF THE ALPHABET   TYPE OF FOOD

Would you rather

have hair that turns _____ whenever you
COLOR

feel _____
ADJECTIVE

or

have eyes that turn _____ whenever
COLOR

you _____ ?
VERB

Would you rather

_____ a steep mountain made of _____
VERB   PLURAL NOUN

or

run across a hot _____ wearing your
NOUN

_____ ?
ARTICLE OF CLOTHING

Would you rather

forget every time you ever _____
                                                    VERB (PAST TENSE)

or

forget all the times you saw _____ ?
                                                    PERSON YOU KNOW

Would you rather

speak _____ languages _____
            NUMBER   ADVERB

or

read other people's _____ ?
                                        PLURAL NOUN

CHOOSE YOUR FATE!

Relax! This is just a game.
Or at least that's what they told you.

Would you rather

have people spread a rumor that you eat _____
PLURAL NOUN

or

have people spread a rumor that you shout

" _____ !" every time you _____ ?
EXCLAMATION   VERB

Would you rather

tell _____ your deepest, darkest secret
PERSON YOU KNOW

about that time you _____
VERB (PAST TENSE)

or

find out _____ 's deepest, darkest secret
CELEBRITY

about their _____ ?
PLURAL NOUN

Would you rather

_____ outside of an airplane with a parachute
VERB

the size of a/an _____
NOUN

or

be stuck at sea in a/an _____ the size of
VEHICLE

a/an _____ ?
NOUN

Would you rather

have _____ forget who you are
PERSON YOU KNOW

or

have _____ know who you are?
CELEBRITY

Would you rather

paint the best _____ in the world
NOUN

or

_____ in the best _____
VERB   ARTICLE OF CLOTHING

in the world?

Would you rather

wake up tomorrow and be the worst in the world

at _____
VERB ENDING IN "ING"

or

wake up tomorrow and be the best in the world

at _____ ?
VERB ENDING IN "ING"

Would you rather

get a tattoo of a/an _____
NOUN

or

get a tattoo of _____ 's face?
PERSON YOU KNOW

Would you rather

always have an extra _____ in your
NOUN

_____
TYPE OF CONTAINER

or

always get to _____ for an extra hour?
VERB

Would you rather

win _____ dollars
NUMBER

or

have your best friend win _____ dollars?
NUMBER

Would you rather

be able to blow a bubble the size of a/an _____
NOUN

or

be able to fold a piece of paper into a/an

_____ ?
SOMETHING ALIVE

Would you rather

be in the history books for your amazing ability

to _____
VERB

or

be in the history books for knowing the most about

_____ ?
PLURAL NOUN

Would you rather

have the ability to communicate with any _____
ANIMAL

or

have the ability to _____ over any _____ ?
VERB   NOUN

Would you rather

have a/an _____ haircut for picture day
ADJECTIVE

or

wear a/an _____ outfit for the first day
ADJECTIVE

of school?

Would you rather

live in a/an _____ -shaped house in _____
NOUN   COUNTRY

or

live in a/an _____ cave in _____ ?
ADJECTIVE   COUNTRY

Would you rather

wear _____ that are too _____
ARTICLE OF CLOTHING (PLURAL)   _ADJECTIVE_

or

wear pants that _____ when you wear them?
VERB

Would you rather

have _____'s wardrobe
CELEBRITY

or

have _____'s hair and makeup team?
CELEBRITY

Would you rather

wear a/an _____ that's itchier than
ARTICLE OF CLOTHING

a/an _____
NOUN

or

wear a hat made of _____
PLURAL NOUN

on your _____ ?
PART OF THE BODY

A CHOOSY DOOZY

Here's some *Would You Rather Mad Libs* that will leave you scratching your head.

Would you rather

wear pajamas with _____'s face on them to
                    CELEBRITY

your _____
         TYPE OF EVENT

or

wear an uncomfortable ball gown to bed for

_____ years?
   NUMBER

Would you rather

read _____
     BOOK TITLE
ten times

or

watch _____
      MOVIE TITLE
twenty times?

Would you rather

have _____ _____
NUMBER   _PLURAL NOUN_

or

_____ one hundred _____ ?
VERB   _TYPE OF BUILDING (PLURAL)_

Would you rather

have everything you eat taste

like _____
TYPE OF FOOD

or

have everything you drink taste like _____ ?
TYPE OF LIQUID

Would you rather

wake up in _____ and not know how to
CITY

_____ with other people
VERB

or

wake up in _____ and not know how to
COUNTRY

_____ your way home?
VERB

Would you rather

go on a world tour with _____ in
CELEBRITY

a/an _____
VEHICLE

or

_____ in a movie with _____ ?
VERB   PERSON YOU KNOW

Would you rather

have _____ forget your birthday
PERSON YOU KNOW

or

forget to go to the _____ of _____ ?
TYPE OF EVENT   PERSON YOU KNOW

Would you rather

be able to run _____
NUMBER

miles per hour

or

be able to _____ _____ times in
VERB   NUMBER

one hour?

◀ 31 ▶

Would you rather

fart _____ whenever you tell a lie
        ADVERB

or

burp whenever you meet a/an _____ person?
                                  ADJECTIVE

Would you rather

unwrap a box of _____ and realize they're
                  PLURAL NOUN

not for you

or

never ever get the _____ you want for
                      NOUN

your _____ ?
      TYPE OF EVENT

Would you rather

get _____ dollars in pennies
      NUMBER

or

get a gift card to _____ for one
                    NAME OF STORE

hundred dollars?

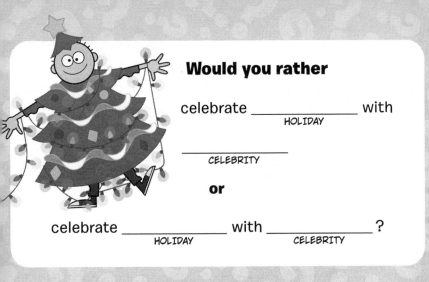

Would you rather

celebrate _____ with
HOLIDAY

_____
CELEBRITY

or

celebrate _____ with _____ ?
HOLIDAY   CELEBRITY

Would you rather

brush your teeth with _____-flavored
TYPE OF FOOD

toothpaste

or

wear perfume that smells like _____ ?
TYPE OF FOOD

Would you rather

be funnier than _____
CELEBRITY

or

be smarter than _____ ?
PERSON FROM HISTORY

Would you rather

be able to _____ the weather
VERB

or

be able to lift _____ using only
PLURAL NOUN

your _____ ?
PART OF THE BODY

Would you rather

live in a historic _____
TYPE OF BUILDING

or

live in _____ 's house?
CELEBRITY

Would you rather

get sucked into _____ and become a
BOOK TITLE

character within it

or

get sucked into _____ and become a
MOVIE TITLE

character within it?

DECISIONS NO ONE SHOULD HAVE TO MAKE

Here's some would-you-rather questions no one should have to answer. But you do!

Would you rather

be an expert at _____ a/an _____
                VERB ENDING IN "ING"   NOUN

or

be average at playing _____ instruments?
                       NUMBER

Would you rather

be able to grant one

_____ wish for yourself
ADJECTIVE

or

be able to grant _____
                  NUMBER

wishes for _____ ?
           PERSON YOU KNOW

Would you rather

grow up to be a/an _____
OCCUPATION

or

grow up to have the same job as _____ ?
PERSON YOU KNOW

Would you rather

have a unicorn named

_____ as your pet
FIRST NAME

or

have a farm full of magical _____ ?
PLURAL NOUN

Would you rather

go hang gliding over a tropical _____
NOUN

or

ride a/an _____ across a/an
VEHICLE

_____ bay?
ADJECTIVE

Would you rather

eat _____ that has been on the counter for
      TYPE OF FOOD

_____ days
      NUMBER

or

drink _____ bathwater?
      ADJECTIVE

Would you rather

own a painting made by _____
                            CELEBRITY

or

own all the _____ ever made by
                PLURAL NOUN

_____ ?
PERSON FROM HISTORY

Would you rather

spend a year living in an igloo in _____
                                      COUNTRY

or

spend a year living in a tent in _____ ?
                                      CITY

Would you rather

give up using your cellular _____ for the
NOUN

rest of your life

or

only be able to use a/an _____ tablet for
NOUN

the rest of your life?

Would you rather

always say "_____, partners!" whenever
EXCLAMATION

you go somewhere

or

always say "_____-loo"
SILLY WORD

whenever you leave

somewhere?

Would you rather

be able to hear a/an _____ drop from
NOUN

_____ miles away
NUMBER

or

be able to _____ faster than
VERB

a robotic _____ ?
NOUN

Would you rather

turn into a/an _____ every full moon
ANIMAL

or

eat like a/an _____
ANIMAL

all the time?

WHEN IN DOUBT, GUESS!

If you're not sure about the answer to these would-you-rather questions, just guess! How bad could it be? GULP!

Would you rather

always hear the sound of someone banging

_____
PLURAL NOUN

or

always hear the sound of someone

_____ ?
VERB ENDING IN "ING"

Would you rather

_____ in front of _____
VERB   PERSON YOU KNOW

or

_____ in the middle of a crowded
VERB

_____ ?
A PLACE

Would you rather

get unlimited money to spend at _____
NAME OF STORE

or

get _____ dollars to spend at _____
NUMBER   NUMBER

different stores?

Would you rather

move around like a/an _____ to get
ANIMAL

where you're going

or

make the same noises as a/an _____
SOMETHING ALIVE

whenever you try to speak?

Would you rather

find out that you just won a new _____
NOUN

or

find out that _____ is coming to visit you?
CELEBRITY

Would you rather

swim in a pool with a hungry _____
ANIMAL

or

have a/an _____
SOMETHING ALIVE

in your bathtub?

Would you rather

give your best friend a lifetime supply of

_____
PLURAL NOUN

or

give _____ unlimited trips to _____?
PERSON YOU KNOW   COUNTRY

Would you rather

cry like a/an _____ when you watch
<u>SOMETHING ALIVE</u>

a/an _____ movie
<u>ADJECTIVE</u>

or

laugh so hard your _____ falls off when
<u>ARTICLE OF CLOTHING</u>

someone _____ a joke?
<u>VERB ENDING IN "S"</u>

Would you rather

spend a day wearing a wet _____
<u>ARTICLE OF CLOTHING</u>

or

wear a/an _____ that is two sizes too
<u>ARTICLE OF CLOTHING</u>

small all day?

CHOOSING ISN'T EASY WHEN YOU'RE FEELING QUEASY!

WARNING: Some questions below may cause not-so-fun side effects! Answer at your own risk!

Would you rather

have your laugh sound like a/an _____
ANIMAL

or

have your laugh make a/an " _____ " sound?
A SOUND

Would you rather

drink a gallon of _____ and then
TYPE OF LIQUID

_____ for a mile
VERB

or

eat enough _____ for _____ people
TYPE OF FOOD   NUMBER

and then ride a roller coaster?

Would you rather

be the size of a/an _____ for a week
                           NOUN

or

be the size of a/an _____ for a week?
                         SOMETHING ALIVE

Would you rather

own a/an _____ that can _____
                VEHICLE   VERB

underwater

or

own a car with its own _____
                                NOUN

launcher?

Would you rather

find the _____ you lost _____ years ago
              NOUN   NUMBER

or

get _____ as a gift from _____?
     PLURAL NOUN   PERSON YOU KNOW

Would you rather

live in a/an _____ house made of _____
ADJECTIVE   PLURAL NOUN

or

live in a/an _____ made from recycled
TYPE OF BUILDING

_____ ?
PLURAL NOUN

Would you rather

live in a/an _____ place with _____
ADJECTIVE   NUMBER

inches of rain per year

or

live in a place with heavy

_____ and lots of
PLURAL NOUN

_____ -storms?
NOUN

Would you rather

eat what a/an _____
ANIMAL

eats for a day

or

eat what _____ eats for a year?
PERSON YOU KNOW

Would you rather

have more feathers than a/an _____
ANIMAL

or

have scalier skin than a/an _____ ?
SOMETHING ALIVE

Would you rather

always have a/an _____ on your face
NOUN

or

have a/an _____ that always looks
PART OF THE BODY

_____ ?
ADJECTIVE

Would you rather

have a/an _____ wand for _____ days
       ADJECTIVE   NUMBER

or

have a/an _____ carpet for
        VERB ENDING IN "ING"

_____ days?
    NUMBER

Would you rather

win an award for being the most _____
                                   ADJECTIVE

kid in school

or

win an award for being the best kid at

_____ in school?
VERB ENDING IN "ING"

Would you rather

have a personal chef that can make

_____ for you anytime you want
TYPE OF FOOD

or

have a tutor who does your

homework, but only _____
NUMBER

times a week?

Would you rather

sprain your _____
PART OF THE BODY

before your sports team's

final game

or

have to wear a cast at your

fifteenth _____ ?
TYPE OF EVENT

Would you rather

_____ a soccer game in flip-flops
VERB

or

play a game of foot- _____ while wearing
NOUN

_____ boots?
ADJECTIVE

Would you rather

be best friends with an alien from the planet

_____
SILLY WORD

or

have a/an _____ alien from outer space as
ADJECTIVE

your _____ ?
OCCUPATION

BETWEEN A ROCK AND A (RATHER) HARD PLACE

Some would-you-rather questions leave you to decide between two bad options. When this happens, do your best and get ready for the funny!

Would you rather

have an embarrassing video of you

_____ go viral
VERB ENDING IN "ING"

or

have a video of you singing " _____ "
SONG TITLE

like a wild _____ go viral?
ANIMAL

Would you rather

have a day where it rains _____
TYPE OF FOOD

or

have a day where it hails _____ ?
PLURAL NOUN

Would you rather

have _____ _____ every
SOMETHING ALIVE (PLURAL)   VERB

time you tell a joke

or

have people _____ on their
VERB

_____ whenever you enter the room?
PART OF THE BODY (PLURAL)

Would you rather

get stuck in an elevator for a day with someone who

is _____
ADJECTIVE

or

get stuck in an elevator for a day with someone

who won't stop _____?
VERB ENDING IN "ING"

Would you rather

find out where the sidewalk _____
VERB ENDING IN "S"

or

find out what's over the _____-bow?
NOUN

Would you rather

go _____ years into the past for a/an
NUMBER

_____ visit
ADJECTIVE

or

go that many years into

the future and _____
VERB

there forever?

Would you rather

have _____ read your

PERSON YOU KNOW

diary entries about your favorite

_____

NOUN

or

have your mom read your

text messages about _____ ?

PLURAL NOUN

Would you rather

live in a house made out of _____

TYPE OF FOOD

or

only be able to bathe in _____ ?

TYPE OF LIQUID

Would you rather

never _____ again

VERB

or

never have a/an _____ again?

TYPE OF EVENT

Would you rather

go on a field trip with your class to a/an

_____ _____
ADJECTIVE   TYPE OF BUILDING

or

go on a trip with your family to _____ to see
                                          CITY

the _____ of Liberty?
          NOUN

Would you rather

have the arms of a/an

_____
ANIMAL

or

have the _____
            PART OF THE BODY (PLURAL)

of a giraffe?

Would you rather

be able to ice- _____ backward
VERB

or

be able to do gymnastics on uneven _____ ?
PLURAL NOUN

Would you rather

switch lives with _____ for a day
CELEBRITY

or

go back in time and spend a day with

_____ ?
PERSON FROM HISTORY

Would you rather

dye your hair _____ for the next ten years
COLOR
.

or

wear a sparkly _____ on your head for the
NOUN

next ten years?

Would you rather

save all your _____ for a/an _____ day
PLURAL NOUN   ADJECTIVE

or

spend all your money as fast as you can

_____ it?
VERB

Would you rather

have fingernails that are _____ inches long
NUMBER

or

have hair that is _____ feet long?
NUMBER

Would you rather

parachute off of a/an _____ that is
TYPE OF BUILDING

_____ stories high
NUMBER

or

sit in a/an _____ in the ocean that's two
TYPE OF CONTAINER

hundred _____ underwater?
PLURAL NOUN

BON VOYAGE!

It's time to go on a vacation! Let's find out where you want to go!

Would you rather

_____ in a/an _____ air balloon
VERB   ADJECTIVE

over _____
COUNTRY

or

take a cruise _____ to the different
VEHICLE

beaches of your favorite _____?
A PLACE

Would you rather

fly for _____ hours on a plane sitting next to
NUMBER

a/an _____ _____
ADJECTIVE   OCCUPATION

or

ride on a train full of _____ across
ANIMAL (PLURAL)

_____?
COUNTRY

Would you rather

go _____ -watching on a boat with
    ANIMAL

_____ as the captain
PERSON YOU KNOW

or

take a tour of a famous _____ with a/an
                        NOUN

_____ you don't trust very much?
OCCUPATION

Would you rather

forget to _____ your bathing suit
          VERB

or

forget to pack your _____ ?
                    NOUN

Would you rather

wear SPF _____ sunscreen only on your
NUMBER

_____
PART OF THE BODY

or

wear a hat that is bigger than a/an _____ ?
NOUN

Would you rather

travel to a/an _____ place you've never been to
ADJECTIVE

or

travel to a/an _____ place that you've been
ADJECTIVE

to _____ times?
NUMBER

Would you rather

have your hotel room smell like moldy _____
PLURAL NOUN

or

have all of your clothes smell like a/an _____
ADJECTIVE

dog?

Would you rather

go _____ in a/an _____ tent
VERB ENDING IN "ING"   ADJECTIVE

or

go camping in a luxury _____ ?
NOUN

Would you rather

go on a/an _____ -mile hike up a steep
NUMBER

_____
NOUN

or

go for a swim in _____ water?
ADJECTIVE

Would you rather

spend the day _____
VERB ENDING IN "ING"

in a/an _____ tub
ADJECTIVE

or

spend the day lounging on a beach _____ in
NOUN

(the) _____ ?
A PLACE

Would you rather

go on a luxury vacation to _____ with your
COUNTRY

teacher

or

go on a staycation in your living room with

_____ ?
PERSON YOU KNOW

Would you rather

go on a/an _____ -week vacation where you
NUMBER

only eat _____
TYPE OF FOOD

or

stay in a hotel for _____
NUMBER

weeks with a roommate who

_____ in their sleep?
VERB ENDING IN "S"

Would you rather

visit _____ new countries in one week
NUMBER

or

spend _____ weeks in one new country?
NUMBER

Would you rather

go to an amusement park but only get to ride

_____ rides
NUMBER

or

go to a/an _____ that only has _____
A PLACE   NUMBER

animals?

Would you rather

visit the biggest _____ in the United States
NOUN

or

visit a house shaped like a/an _____?
NOUN

Would you rather

visit an ancient pyramid that was built by

_____
OCCUPATION (PLURAL)

or

visit a museum that has a collection of priceless

_____ ?
PLURAL NOUN

Would you rather

travel to a/an _____ amusement park to
ADJECTIVE

meet _____ _____
FIRST NAME   ANIMAL

or

visit _____ -sburg, a town that feels like it's
LAST NAME

from _____ years in the
NUMBER

past?

SUMMER CAMP OR BUMMER CAMP

Your parents are going to send you to summer camp this year! But will you like it?

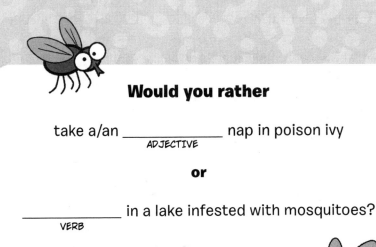

Would you rather

take a/an _____ nap in poison ivy
ADJECTIVE

or

_____ in a lake infested with mosquitoes?
VERB

Would you rather

lose your map of all the _____ trails in
VERB ENDING IN "ING"

the forest

or

lose your magnetic _____ in the forest?
NOUN

Would you rather

find lots of tiny _____ in your sleeping bag
ANIMAL (PLURAL)

or

hear one huge _____
ANIMAL

outside your tent?

Would you rather

_____ on a rope into a lake
VERB

or

sail a/an _____ on a lake?
VEHICLE

Would you rather

make a friendship _____ out of string, beads,
NOUN

and _____
PLURAL NOUN

or

shoot arrows using a wooden _____ ?
NOUN

Would you rather

share a tent with a/an _____ who

OCCUPATION

_____ all night

VERB ENDING IN "S"

or

share a cabin with twelve _____ in a

OCCUPATION (PLURAL)

marching band?

Would you rather

give out _____ friendship bracelets to other

NUMBER

campers

or

receive _____ friendship bracelets from other

NUMBER

campers?

Would you rather

have to eat _____ every day, all summer,
TYPE OF FOOD

or

have to wear the same _____
ARTICLE OF CLOTHING

every day, all summer?

Would you rather

get woken up every day by the sound of a/an

_____ screaming
ANIMAL

or

fall asleep to the sound of your bunkmate

_____ a tuba?
VERB ENDING IN "ING"

Would you rather

start a campfire using only _____ and sticks
PLURAL NOUN

or

start a campfire using flint and some _____ ?
PLURAL NOUN

Would you rather

ride a/an _____ down the rapids
NOUN

or

fend for yourself against a/an _____
ANIMAL

in the woods?

UH-OH

Would you rather

play tug-of-war against _____
CELEBRITY

or

run a race with your _____ tied to
PART OF THE BODY

_____ ?
PERSON YOU KNOW

Would you rather

share a teeny tent with _____
CELEBRITY

or

share a whole cabin with _____?
PERSON YOU KNOW

Would you rather

get a sunburn shaped like a/an _____ on
NOUN

your forehead

or

get a tummy ache because you ate too many

_____ s'mores?
TYPE OF FOOD

Would you rather

spend the afternoon _____ in the forest

VERB ENDING IN "ING"

or

spend the evening listening to

_____ stories about

ADJECTIVE

haunted _____ ?

PLURAL NOUN

Would you rather

be assigned the camp nickname " _____

ADJECTIVE

_____ "

NOUN

or

have everyone call you the name of your celebrity

look-alike, _____ ?

CELEBRITY

Would you rather

take a shower and discover that a/an _____
ANIMAL

has stolen your towel

or

find out your toothbrush was used to clean the

_____ ?
TYPE OF FURNITURE

Would you rather

accidentally lose a/an _____ note you wrote
ADJECTIVE

to _____
PERSON YOU KNOW

or

listen to a ghost story that makes you scream

" _____ "?
EXCLAMATION

WELCOME TO THE PET PLACE

Animal lovers unite! Here are some quirky questions about all kinds of cuddly critters.

Would you rather

find out your dog drooled on your favorite

_____
ARTICLE OF CLOTHING

or

find out your dog _____ your homework?
VERB (PAST TENSE)

Would you rather

have a puppy that grows up to be the size of

a race- _____
ANIMAL

or

have a racehorse that's smaller than a/an

_____ ?
NOUN

Would you rather

get a/an _____ kitten named _____
             COLOR   SILLY WORD

or

get a/an _____ kitten named _____ ?
       ADJECTIVE   TYPE OF FOOD

Would you rather

get a/an _____-eating dinosaur as a pet
          NOUN

or

get a/an _____ octopus as a pet?
         ADJECTIVE

Would you rather

have a dog who needs to be walked _____
                                    NUMBER

times a day

or

have a cat who always scratches your

_____ ?
PART OF THE BODY

Would you rather

have a tarantula that sneaks out of its

_____
TYPE OF CONTAINER

or

have a parrot that tosses its _____
TYPE OF FOOD (PLURAL)

on the floor?

Would you rather

get a fluffy puppy that likes to _____
VERB

or

get a/an _____ lizard that would rather
ADJECTIVE

cuddle with a hot _____ ?
NOUN

Would you rather

groom your dog with a/an _____
NOUN

or

brush your dog's _____ with a toothbrush?
PART OF THE BODY

Would you rather

have a pet that makes a/an "_____" sound
SILLY WORD

when it snores

or

have a pet that sounds like a/an _____ when
NOUN

it snores?

Would you rather

adopt the dog that gives you too many _____
PLURAL NOUN

or

adopt the dog that is always _____
VERB ENDING IN "ING"

on the floor?

Would you rather

have _____ guinea pigs
NUMBER

or

have one actual pig with a cute _____ tail?
COLOR

Would you rather

get a goldfish that _____
VERB ENDING IN "S"

back and forth in its tank

or

get a turtle that _____ on a rock all day?
VERB ENDING IN "S"

Would you rather

have a/an _____ bunny with
ADJECTIVE

_____-inch-long teeth as a pet
NUMBER

or

have a scaly _____ with _____ eyes
ANIMAL   COLOR

as a pet?

Would you rather

dress your hamster up in a/an _____
ARTICLE OF CLOTHING

or

paint a picture of your turtle _____?
VERB ENDING IN "ING"

Would you rather

find a dolphin in your _____
TYPE OF CONTAINER

or

find a/an _____ in your _____ ?
ANIMAL   A PLACE

Would you rather

let your tarantula crawl on your _____
PART OF THE BODY

or

let your snake _____
VERB

around your arm?

Would you rather

adopt a/an _____-fish with _____ eyes
COLOR   ADJECTIVE

or

adopt a hermit crab that lives inside a/an

_____ ?
NOUN

ONE-STAR RESTAURANT

Order up! Time to eat at the best restaurant in town (if you dare).

Would you rather

eat a/an _____ sandwich sprinkled with
TYPE OF FOOD

_____ from the floor
PLURAL NOUN

or

eat a cheese sandwich sprinkled with _____
COLOR

dryer lint?

Would you rather

enjoy a/an _____ that was in the trash for
TYPE OF FOOD

a week

or

eat a slice of _____ pizza that has ants on it?
TYPE OF FOOD

Would you rather

eat a deep-fried _____
NOUN

or

eat a deep-fried _____ ?
SOMETHING ALIVE

Would you rather

dine at a restaurant inside a/an _____
VEHICLE

that's _____ miles under the ocean
NUMBER

or

dine at a restaurant in a rocket ship shaped like a/an

_____ that's orbiting (the) _____ ?
NOUN   A PLACE

Would you rather

eat _____ and onions every day for a year
TYPE OF FOOD

or

eat a jar full of pickled _____ in one day?
PLURAL NOUN

Would you rather

eat a birthday cake

that tastes like wet

_____
PLURAL NOUN

or

eat a/an _____ covered in sauerkraut?
TYPE OF FOOD

Would you rather

order lunch from a chef who only cooks using

a/an _____
NOUN

or

order lunch from a/an _____ who only cooks
OCCUPATION

food that tastes _____?
ADJECTIVE

Would you rather

give up _____ forever
TYPE OF DESSERT

or

give up _____ forever?
TYPE OF BEVERAGE

Would you rather

have to dip everything you eat in _____
PLURAL NOUN

or

have to _____ cinnamon on everything
VERB

you eat?

Would you rather

eat ravioli stuffed with _____
TYPE OF FOOD

or

eat pizza with _____ on top?
TYPE OF FOOD

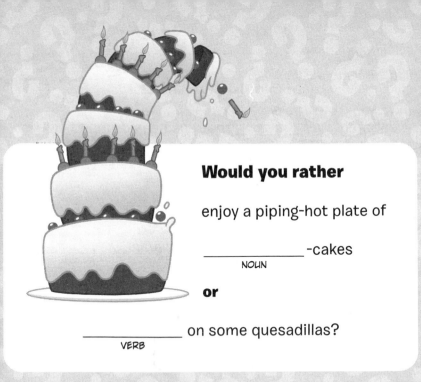

Would you rather

enjoy a piping-hot plate of

_____ -cakes
NOUN

or

_____ on some quesadillas?
VERB

Would you rather

have a cup of soup made of _____ and
TYPE OF LIQUID

_____
PLURAL NOUN

or

have a/an _____ -shake
NOUN

made of _____ ice cream?
NOUN

Would you rather

eat a/an _____ that has been dropped on the
           TYPE OF FOOD

floor of (the) _____
                  A PLACE

or

drink a/an _____ after a/an _____
              TYPE OF BEVERAGE   ANIMAL

took a slurp?

Would you rather

have to finish eating a sandwich as tall as

(the) _____
        FAMOUS BUILDING

or

have to finish eating _____ cakes in
                          NUMBER

_____ minutes?
    NUMBER

Would you rather

drink a smoothie that makes your _____
PART OF THE BODY

squeak for a week

or

eat a bag of chips that makes you _____
ADJECTIVE

for a week?

Would you rather

eat an apple that makes you

_____ nonstop for a day
VERB

or

eat an orange that makes your hair _____
COLOR

for a month?

Would you rather

chomp a/an _____ -size plate of _____
                 NOUN   PLURAL NOUN

or

sip on a/an _____ full of
             TYPE OF CONTAINER

_____ water?
VERB ENDING IN "ING"

Would you rather

eat a bowl of soup that is _____ degrees
                          NUMBER

or

eat a/an _____ that is still
             TYPE OF FOOD

_____ -percent frozen?
    NUMBER

Would you rather

only be able to eat pizza that has _____ as
TYPE OF FOOD

its topping

or

only be able to eat cake that has _____
TYPE OF FOOD

frosting on it?

Would you rather

have to eat everything using a pair of _____
PLURAL NOUN

or

have to eat everything using your

_____?
PART OF THE BODY (PLURAL)

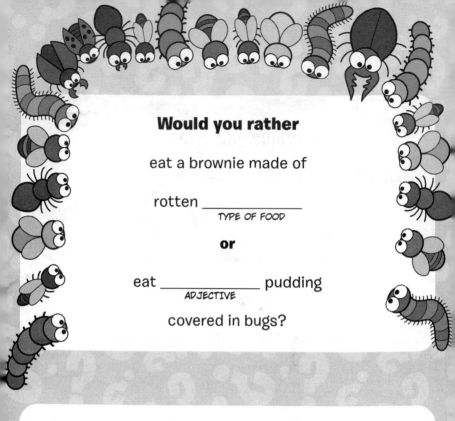

Would you rather

eat a brownie made of

rotten _____
<u>TYPE OF FOOD</u>

or

eat _____ pudding
<u>ADJECTIVE</u>

covered in bugs?

Would you rather

drink water out of your pet _____'s
<u>ANIMAL</u>

water bowl

or

accidentally inhale a/an _____ that's
<u>ANIMAL</u>

flying around?

HAUNTINGLY HORRIFIC DECISIONS

Get ready for some spine-chilling choices that are bound to make you go "Eeeek!"

Would you rather

live in a/an _____ haunted by the ghost
TYPE OF BUILDING

of _____
CELEBRITY

or

stay in a hotel for a week that is haunted by

_____ ghosts?
NUMBER

Would you rather

scream "_____" after seeing a/an
EXCLAMATION

_____ with no head
SOMETHING ALIVE

or

scream like a/an _____ after seeing a
NOUN

floating _____ with huge fangs?
NOUN

Would you rather

have a portrait of a person on your wall whose

_____ always follow you
PART OF THE BODY (PLURAL)

or

have a/an _____ that
INSTRUMENT

eerily plays on its own . . .

but it only plays

" _____ "?
SONG TITLE

Would you rather

have a/an _____ ghost that follows
ADJECTIVE

you around

or

have a ghost trapped in your house who won't

stop _____ ?
VERB ENDING IN "ING"

Would you rather

have a ghostly pet _____
ANIMAL

or

have a ghostly best friend with a bad _____?
NOUN

Would you rather

live in a/an _____ that oozes
TYPE OF BUILDING

_____ slime from the walls
ADJECTIVE

or

live in a house that always has _____
ANIMAL (PLURAL)

crawling on the walls?

Would you rather

spend the night in a haunted house with

_____
PERSON YOU KNOW

or

spend the night in a cemetery with _____?
CELEBRITY

Would you rather

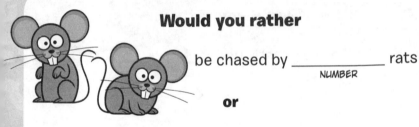

be chased by _____ rats
NUMBER

or

have to fight off one snake the size of a/an

_____ ?
NOUN

Would you rather

share a camp cabin with _____ goblins
NUMBER

or

share a/an _____ with lots of
TYPE OF BUILDING

_____ witches?
ADJECTIVE

Would you rather

be able to _____ with undead spirits
VERB

or

be able to see the ghosts of every _____ ?
SOMETHING ALIVE

Would you rather

find the skeleton of a/an _____ living in
SOMETHING ALIVE

your _____
TYPE OF CONTAINER

or

find out you have a/an _____ monster living
ADJECTIVE

under your _____?
NOUN

Would you rather

have a ghost yell " _____ !" at you whenever
EXCLAMATION

you walk through your front door

or

constantly hear two ghosts whispering about who

_____ in
VERB (PAST TENSE)

your bathroom?

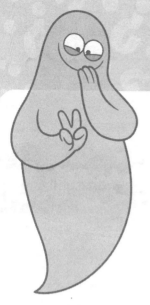

Would you rather

share a bunk bed with a

ghost who talks about

_____ A LOT
VERB ENDING IN "ING"

or

have a ghost in your closet who tears holes in your

_____ ?
ARTICLE OF CLOTHING (PLURAL)

Would you rather

hear a mysterious sound that goes " _____ "
A SOUND

or

hear the sound of _____ clanking
PLURAL NOUN

in the basement?

Would you rather

sleep in a coffin with a massive _____
TYPE OF BUG

or

sleep hanging upside down next to lots

of _____ ?
ANIMAL (PLURAL)

Would you rather

live with a ghost who sings constantly and sounds

like _____
CELEBRITY

or

live with a ghost who keeps knocking over

your _____ ?
PLURAL NOUN

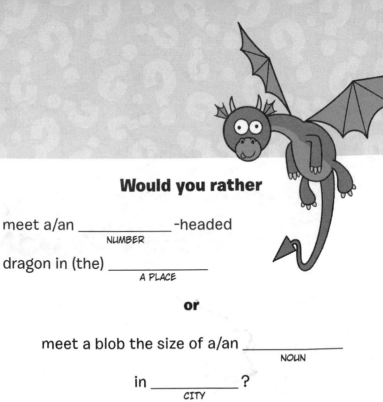

Would you rather

meet a/an _____ -headed
              NUMBER

dragon in (the) _____
              A PLACE

or

meet a blob the size of a/an _____
                          NOUN

in _____ ?
        CITY

Would you rather

have _____ ghosts throw a/an _____
       NUMBER   ADJECTIVE

party in your house

or

have a ghost who keeps drawing heart-shaped

_____ on your walls in blood?
PLURAL NOUN

Would you rather

run a day-scare (a daycare for baby ghosts)

with _____
PERSON YOU KNOW

or

have your hair done by a ghost who only knows

hairstyles from _____ years ago?
NUMBER

Would you rather

live with a/an _____ ghost who used to be
ADJECTIVE

a/an _____
OCCUPATION

or

live in a cemetery and

hear a ghost child

_____ all night?
VERB ENDING IN "ING"

MACHINE MISHAPS

You look like a talented inventor. Let's see what you'd like to create.

Would you rather

have a robot that _____
VERB ENDING IN "S"

or

have a robot that teaches

people how to _____?
VERB

Would you rather

design a machine that helps people _____
VERB

or

make a machine that makes _____ in
TYPE OF FOOD

_____ seconds?
NUMBER

Would you rather

design a machine that you wear on your

_____ to make you _____ faster
PART OF THE BODY   VERB

or

design a new _____ that transports you
ARTICLE OF CLOTHING

to _____ ?
CITY

Would you rather

craft a machine that makes new clothes in

_____ days
NUMBER

or

make a machine that cleans the house super

_____ ?
ADVERB

Would you rather

invent a robot that says, " _____ , it's nice

EXCLAMATION

to _____ you!"

VERB

or

invent a robot that only talks by saying,

" _____ , _____ "?

A SOUND   SAME SOUND

Would you rather

invent a bow and _____ that makes people

NOUN

_____ in love

VERB

or

invent a laser pointer that makes people

_____ like a/an _____ ?

VERB   ANIMAL

Would you rather

craft a machine that makes _____
NUMBER

_____ every time you give it a gallon
PLURAL NOUN

of _____
TYPE OF LIQUID

or

craft a teeny machine that can do the job of a/an

_____ _____ times faster?
OCCUPATION   NUMBER

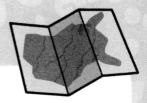

Would you rather

design a teleportation machine that takes you

wherever you want to go in seconds, but you get a/an

_____ -ache every time you use it
PART OF THE BODY

or

design a machine that makes you super strong,

but it makes your face _____ every time
ADJECTIVE

you use it?

Would you rather

have a robot version of _____
PERSON YOU KNOW

or

have a robot version of _____ ?
CELEBRITY

Would you rather

invent a machine that does your homework but gets

_____ percent of the answers wrong
NUMBER

or

invent a machine that cleans your _____
TYPE OF BUILDING

but breaks _____ items?
NUMBER

Would you rather

have a robot that runs on _____
PLURAL NOUN

or

have a robot that runs on _____ ?
TYPE OF LIQUID

Would you rather

own a machine that has _____

_____

or

own a machine that can _____ on any

surface?

Would you rather

invent a machine that can capture the energy of

a/an _____

or

invent a machine that runs on

_____?

WARNING

Would you rather

create a machine that makes all vegetables taste

like _____
    TYPE OF FOOD

or

create a machine that makes all drinks taste

like _____ ?
    TYPE OF LIQUID

Would you rather

switch out your _____ for a superstrong
              PART OF THE BODY

robot one

or

have a robot brain that is _____ times
                          NUMBER

smarter than you?

Would you rather

build a jetpack that makes you fly _____
ADVERB

or

create a/an _____ you can eat to make you
NOUN

look _____ ?
ADJECTIVE

Would you rather

have a robot named _____ Prime
FIRST NAME

or

have a robot named

_____-2-D2?
LETTER OF THE ALPHABET

WELCOME TO THE DISASTER ZONE

When disaster strikes, you've got some big decisions to make!

Would you rather

put out a house fire with a/an _____
TYPE OF CONTAINER

full of water

or

survive an earthquake by hiding under

a/an _____ ?
NOUN

Would you rather

stay safe in a flood by _____ on
VERB ENDING IN "ING"

a/an _____
NOUN

or

escape a tornado while driving a/an _____
VEHICLE

that's running low on gas?

Would you rather

fight in a zombie apocalypse

with only a/an _____
NOUN

as your weapon

or

have _____ turn into
PERSON YOU KNOW

a zombie?

Would you rather

live in a town where everyone gets a disease that

causes nonstop _____
VERB ENDING IN "ING"

or

live in a town where everyone gets a/an

_____ rash that gives them _____
ADJECTIVE   PLURAL NOUN

all over their _____ ?
PART OF THE BODY

Would you rather

wake up one day and find out

_____ is a
PERSON YOU KNOW

were- _____
SOMETHING ALIVE

or

wake up one day and notice that your

_____ has disappeared?
PART OF THE BODY

Would you rather

have to hide in a cave all alone for _____ days
NUMBER

after a/an _____ crashes into the planet
NOUN

or

not be alone but have to share your only

_____ with _____ ?
TYPE OF FOOD   PERSON YOU KNOW

Would you rather

be chased by a flock of _____ that have

ANIMAL (PLURAL)

turned on the human race

or

be chased by a/an _____ vampire through a

ADJECTIVE

dark _____ ?

TYPE OF BUILDING

Would you rather

have a spaceship the size of a/an _____ land

NOUN

on your house

or

have lava flood the floor of your _____ ?

TYPE OF BUILDING

Would you rather

run away from mummies wearing _____
ADJECTIVE

shoes that are _____ sizes too small
NUMBER

or

fight off mummies with only a/an _____ to
NOUN

help you?

Would you rather

have to eat a/an _____ during the
ANIMAL

apocalypse to survive

or

have to fight _____ over
PERSON YOU KNOW

a cart of groceries to survive?

Would you rather

get abducted by _____ aliens that want to
ADJECTIVE

study how you _____
VERB

or

have your body taken over by _____
SOMETHING ALIVE (PLURAL)

but receive the power to _____ better than
VERB

any human on Earth?

Would you rather

go over a waterfall in a/an _____
TYPE OF CONTAINER

or

be at the bottom of a dam when it

_____?
VERB ENDING IN "S"

Would you rather

wear a very loud _____ while sneaking
ARTICLE OF CLOTHING

away from _____ trolls
ADJECTIVE

or

_____ yourself using only a/an _____
VERB   NOUN

against angry trolls?

Would you rather

get bitten by a/an _____ zombie
ADJECTIVE

or

get bitten on the _____ by a vampire?
PART OF THE BODY

DREAM JOB OR JOB NIGHTMARE

Everyone is great at doing something!
Answer these questions to find out what jobs
are right for you!

Would you rather

be a construction worker who builds things out

of _____
PLURAL NOUN

or

be a doctor who operates using your

_____ ?
PART OF THE BODY (PLURAL)

Would you rather

take care of _____ baby _____
NUMBER   ANIMAL (PLURAL)

or

teach _____-year-old children to
NUMBER

ice- _____ ?
VERB

Would you rather

be a/an _____ who competes
OCCUPATION

in the Olympics

or

be a professional _____ -ball
NOUN

coach who goes to the

_____ Bowl?
ADJECTIVE

Would you rather

get paid _____ _____ every hour
NUMBER   TYPE OF FOOD (PLURAL)

or

get paid one hundred _____ every
PLURAL NOUN

_____ days?
NUMBER

Would you rather

drive a/an _____ to deliver _____
VEHICLE   TYPE OF FOOD (PLURAL)

or

drive a/an _____ van to deliver
VERB ENDING IN "ING"

_____ ?
PLURAL NOUN

Would you rather

work as a conductor who drives a/an

_____ -speed _____
ADJECTIVE   VEHICLE

or

work as a conductor who leads a chorus of singing

_____ ?
SOMETHING ALIVE (PLURAL)

Would you rather

be a/an _____ rescue expert
<small>ANIMAL</small>

or

drive a sled that's pulled

by _____?
<small>ANIMAL (PLURAL)</small>

Would you rather

play professional _____ hockey on
<small>ADJECTIVE</small>

_____'s team
<small>CELEBRITY</small>

or

_____ in a rock concert with
<small>VERB</small>

_____?
<small>PERSON YOU KNOW</small>

Would you rather

be a scientist who _____
                        VERB ENDING IN "S"

lava in a real volcano

or

be a/an _____ who digs for _____
            OCCUPATION   NOUN

nuggets underground?

Would you rather

play a/an _____ _____ in a
              ADJECTIVE   SOMETHING ALIVE

Broadway musical

or

star in a movie about a/an

_____ who likes
   OCCUPATION

to _____?
        VERB

Would you rather

_____ _____ in their natural habitat
VERB   ANIMAL (PLURAL)

or

ride a/an _____ _____ at the rodeo?
VERB ENDING IN "ING"   ANIMAL

Would you rather

get a summer job working in a/an _____
TYPE OF BUILDING

with no air- _____
VERB ENDING IN "ING"

or

get a summer job working as a/an _____ in
OCCUPATION

a tiny _____?
TYPE OF BUILDING

Would you rather

be the first astronaut to land on (the) _____
                                              A PLACE

or

be the first race-car driver to go _____ miles
                                          NUMBER

per hour?

Would you rather

be a/an _____ spy who has to parachute out
            ADJECTIVE

of their _____
              VEHICLE

or

be an undercover _____ who hides in
                        OCCUPATION

a/an _____ ?
         TYPE OF CONTAINER

Would you rather

babysit _____ babies who cry _____
NUMBER ADVERB

or

dog-sit _____ puppies who chew on your
NUMBER

_____ ?
PLURAL NOUN

Would you rather

be a famous clown named _____ the Clown
VERB ENDING IN "S"

or

be a famous author named Dr. _____ ?
SILLY WORD

Would you rather

test-ride a new roller coaster that is taller than

a/an _____
TYPE OF BUILDING

or

taste-test a new BBQ sauce that is hotter than spicy

_____ ?
TYPE OF FOOD (PLURAL)

Would you rather

own a business that makes _____
ADJECTIVE

_____
PLURAL NOUN

or

own a business that makes _____
ADJECTIVE

_____ ?
ARTICLE OF CLOTHING (PLURAL)

Would you rather

go to school for _____ years to be
NUMBER

a/an _____
OCCUPATION

or

go to (the) _____ to become
A PLACE

a/an _____ ?
OCCUPATION

Would you rather

invent a robot _____ that can _____
OCCUPATION   VERB

your dirty laundry

or

design a/an _____ -powered jet
NOUN

_____ that flies you to school?
VEHICLE

Would you rather

be an explorer in an ancient _____ filled with
A PLACE

poisonous _____
SOMETHING ALIVE

or

be a lifeguard at a beach with _____ -foot
NUMBER

waves?

WITH GREAT POWER COMES GREAT SILLINESS

You wake up one day with new super (and not-so-super) abilities! Would you rather . . .

Would you rather

have the power to _____ objects with your
VERB

eyes for one year

or

be able to _____ tall
VERB

_____ forever?
TYPE OF BUILDING (PLURAL)

Would you rather

have all of the powers of a jungle _____
ANIMAL

or

have all of the powers of an underwater

_____ ?
SOMETHING ALIVE

Would you rather

fight crime in _____ as _____'s

CITY   CELEBRITY

sidekick

or

take over (the) _____ with a/an _____

A PLACE   ADJECTIVE

villain?

Would you rather

be strong enough to lift a/an _____

NOUN

or

be faster than a/an _____ ?

VEHICLE

Would you rather

shoot _____ out of your hands

PLURAL NOUN

or

have _____-control powers?

PART OF THE BODY

Would you rather

save the _____ with the help of _____
       NOUN   NUMBER

superheroes

or

save the _____ with a sidekick named
       NOUN

_____ ?
   SILLY WORD

Would you rather

have the power to _____ because you got
                        VERB

bit by a radioactive _____
                           ANIMAL

or

have the power to shoot

_____ blasts
   NOUN

because you fell in a vat

of toxic _____ ?
         TYPE OF LIQUID

Would you rather

hide your superhero identity by pretending to be a/an

_____ _____
ADJECTIVE　　　　　　OCCUPATION

or

hide your superhero identity by pretending to work in

a/an _____ ?
TYPE OF BUILDING

Would you rather

have the ability to _____
VERB

underwater

or

have a super suit with

_____ gadgets?
NUMBER

Would you rather

be a superhero named The _____ _____
COLOR   ANIMAL

or

be a supervillain named _____-man?
ADJECTIVE

Would you rather

team up with a superhero named Wonder

_____
SOMETHING ALIVE

or

team up with a supervillain named The

_____-er?
VERB

Would you rather

have _____ as your sidekick
PERSON YOU KNOW

or

be the sidekick of _____?
CELEBRITY

Would you rather

wear a superhero mask on your _____
PART OF THE BODY

or

wear a/an _____ superhero cape that can
COLOR

make you _____ ?
VERB

Would you rather

lose the ability to _____ whenever you're
VERB

near _____
PLURAL NOUN

or

lose the ability to fly

whenever someone says

" _____ "?
EXCLAMATION